TRIBAL SOVEREIGNTY:
THE RIGHT TO SELF-RULE

Gary Robinson

DEDICATION

This book is dedicated to generations of American Indians who kept tribal identity and sovereignty alive in the face of overwhelming odds.

NOTE TO READERS

This little booklet accompanies and expands on my previously produced educational DVD of the same title. Both the DVD and the book were created to increase the general public's awareness of this little known or understood topic. It should be taught in every school and college in the U.S. because tribal governments and tribal sovereignty are historical and legal facts of life. Yet, countless numbers of non-Indian communities continually display their ignorance of this subject in word and deed. May more and more people eventually "get it."

FOREWORD

I strongly recommend this booklet for classroom use. While Native American tribes are sometimes in the news because of casinos, the general public poorly understands the historical reasons and legal realities behind their special relationship to the United States government. And in high schools and even universities, students are exposed to little information about tribal sovereignty and related social and political issues. This concise, clear, and comprehensive piece explains the concept of sovereignty and its historical basis in relation to tribes, cities, counties, states and the federal government. It explains why Indian tribes have a different legal and political status than other "minority" groups, why Native Americans have dual citizenship (as U.S. citizens and as members of their tribes), and the legal difference between the more than 560 federally recognized tribes and other tribes within the United States. Reviewing important Supreme Court decisions and acts passed by Congress, this booklet traces the development of tribes from their first encounters with Europeans to the present. First dealt with as preexisting tribal nations with their own governments by the Europeans, this booklet explains why federally recognized tribes are today understood as domestic sovereign self-governing nations that enjoy a nation-to-nation relationship with the U.S government. This piece also addresses many myths regarding tribal gaming, the taxes paid by Native Americans, and the purpose of revenues generated by Indian casinos. Informative and to the point, Tribal Sovereignty is ideal for classroom use and for anyone interested in learning more about this important contemporary topic.

Paul H. Gelles, Ph.D.

INTRODUCTION

Most Americans are unaware of the unique political status held by American Indian tribes and the special relationship that exists between tribes and the United States government. The concept of <u>sovereignty</u> is the foundation upon which this status and this relationship are built. In these pages we'll examine some of the most common questions and misconceptions people have about tribal governments, how they originated and what empowers them.

(NOTE: In this work, the terms "Native American," "American Indian" and "Indian" are used interchangeably, the same way these terms are often used within American Indian communities.)

NATIVE AMERICAN TRIBAL GOVERNMENTS

First of all, it's important to establish a fact of which many Americans are unaware: in addition to being citizens of the United States, American Indian <u>individuals</u> are also members of <u>tribes</u>, and Native American tribes are political groups ruled by their own <u>governments</u>. *In fact, tribal governments are the oldest governments in the Western Hemisphere.*

But most people in the U.S. don't have a background in American Indian history or American Indian policy. We're not taught any of this in our high schools or even in college courses. So let's repeat the fact. Politically speaking, Indian tribes are governments.

Even understanding that is difficult for some, because here in the United States we have an "ethnic group" model, or an "immigrant model," that teaches us to think of ethnicities. For example, we talk about African Americans, Italian Americans, Irish Americans, and then we use the term Native Americans. However, that term really has additional dimensions of meaning not found in the other ethnic labels and that dimension involves multiple citizenships. Native Americans may be citizens of a county, a city, a state, a tribe and the United States.

As a matter of fact, tribal governments are one of the <u>four types</u> of federally recognized governments in the United States. These are: 1) City governments, 2) County governments, 3) State governments and 4) Tribal governments. American Indians are unique in that they really have <u>dual</u> citizenship, both as citizens of the United States and as citizens of their own tribal nations. And, as this continent's first inhabitants, American Indians are unique in other ways as well.

According to anthropologists and Indians, American Indians are the original people of this land. We know from archaeological evidence that Indians have been here in North America at least 13,000 years, and perhaps even longer. Human remains discovered on one of the Channel Islands near Santa Barbara, California, have been dated as being that old. And the tribes that exist today are descended from those first people.

From the beginning of contact with European immigrants on this continent's east coast, American Indian tribes were considered to be nations, nations that exercised sovereignty. France, England and other European nations entered into treaties with these Indian nations on a government-to-government basis.

So, while individual Indians are mostly like everybody else in the country, they are also citizens of pre-existing tribal nations, and those nations have certain powers and rights recognized, as we'll see, by the U.S. Constitution and Supreme Court. So, to reiterate, American Indians are considered to be pre-existing peoples ruled by their own governments, which qualifies them to be called nations.

WHAT IS SOVEREIGNTY?

Legitimate governments rule on the basis of their sovereignty. So what is sovereignty and how does this concept relate to Native American tribes? In 2004, President George Bush famously fumbled through an attempted answer to this very question. "Tribal sovereignty means that," he told Native American journalist Mark Trahant. "It's sovereign. You're a ... you're a ... you've been given sovereignty, and you're viewed as a sovereign entity." It was a little humorous at the time, but also sad. Sad because it reflects the same confusion most Americans have about this aspect of their own history and social structure.

Simply put, sovereignty is the internationally recognized power of a nation to govern itself, and American Indian tribes existed as sovereign governments long before Europeans settled here. Treaties between European powers, and later the United States, formalized this nation-to-nation relationship between these powers and Indian tribes.

Even the U.S. Constitution recognizes Indian tribes as distinct governments. Article 1, Section 8, of the Constitution specifies that Congress shall regulate commerce with and enter into treaties with "foreign nations, the several states, and with Indian tribes." The legal definition of treaty is an agreement in written form between nation states that is intended to establish a relationship governed by international law.

However, for most American Indians sovereignty is a living relationship between the people, the land they live on and their right to determination how they use that land.

TRUST RESPONSIBILITY

By making treaties with the United States, Native Americans agreed to give up certain rights in exchange for promises from the federal government. These promises, considered by Indians to be sacred perpetual agreements, included the right to education and health care, hunting and fishing rights, the rights to live on land called reservations, and others. <u>Trust responsibility</u> is the term used to describe the government's obligation to honor these promises, which boil down to a promise to protect the best interests of the tribes and their members *forever*.

THE SUPREME COURT'S ROLE

The role of the Supreme Court in affecting Indian sovereignty is best understood in relation to the powers of Congress and the state governments. Under the Constitution, Congress has the power and duty to regulate commerce with the Indian tribes. During the 1800s, the rights of individual Indians and their governments were put to the test in the U.S. legal system. Three landmark Supreme Court decisions from that time period serve as the cornerstone for the continued sovereign status of Indian nations.

The first case, <u>Johnson vs. McIntosh</u> (1823), concerned the validity of a tribal land grant made to private individuals. In this case, the court ruled that tribal rights to sovereignty had been impaired by colonization but not disregarded, and held that the federal government alone has the right to negotiate for American Indian land, not individuals.

In the case known as the <u>Cherokee Nation vs. Georgia</u> (1831), the Cherokee Tribe of Indians sued the state of Georgia because that state had assumed powers it didn't have when it seized tribal lands. In it's ruling in favor of the tribe, the Supreme Court described Indian tribes as "domestic dependent nations" and maintained that the federal-tribal relationship "resembles that of a ward to his guardian."

The <u>Worcester vs. Georgia</u> case of 1832 concerned the application of Georgia state law within the Cherokee Nation reservation. This Supreme Court decision established three things: 1) Tribes did not lose their sovereign powers by becoming subject to the power of the United States, 2) Only Congress has plenary, or overriding, power over Indian affairs, and 3) State laws <u>do not</u> apply in Indian Country (a common term referring to Indian reservation lands.)

FEDERALLY RECOGNIZED TRIBES

The powers and rights discussed here apply only to
<u>federally recognized tribes</u>. Many groups and sub-
groups of Indians exist in the U.S. boundaries, but not
all have established their own independent relationship
to the federal government. Managed by the
Department of the Interior, the U.S. government
maintains a specific set of criteria used to determine if a
tribe falls into the nation-to-nation relationship. The
federal recognition application is a grueling process that
can take from ten to twenty years to achieve. As of
2015, there were approximately 560 federally
recognized Indian tribes in the U.S.

LIMITATIONS TO TRIBAL SOVEREIGNTY

Over the years, Congress has passed laws that have modified the powers of tribes and further defined their nation-to-nation relationship with the federal government. However, the Supreme Court has determined to what degree tribal sovereignty can be modified by Congress.

The first law came in 1934 when Congress passed the **Indian Reorganization Act**. This law reversed trends that had been set in motion in the 1890s that progressively stripped tribes of their rights to self-government and self-management of local assets. The Indian Reorganization Act, known as the I.R.A., established standardized tribal political structures for tribes that wish to deal with the federal government, creating the elected tribal council structure, which is still employed by many tribes today.

In 1953 Congress enacted **Public Law 83-280** to grant certain states criminal jurisdiction over American Indians on reservations and to allow civil litigation that had come under tribal or federal jurisdiction to be handled by state courts. However, the law did not grant states regulatory power over tribes or lands held in trust by the federal government. It also federally guaranteed tribal hunting, trapping and fishing rights and defined basic tribal government functions such as enrollment of members and domestic relations. It prevented states from imposing state taxes on tribes as well as denying states the right to regulate environmental matters, land use, gambling and licensing within reservations.

The **Indian Self-Determination Act** of 1975 made it possible for many tribes to become more self-governing by contracting with the federal government to run their own health-care and social service programs. Previously, many of these services were administered by the Bureau of Indian Affairs, a department within the Department of the Interior. These tribally-operated programs have to meet certain standards and requirements in order to remain under control of the tribe.

In 1978, Congress passed the **Indian Child Welfare Act**, which established procedures state agencies and courts must follow in handling Indian child custody matters. Until passage of this law, outside social and religious organizations routinely took charge of Native American children without regard for tribal culture or social values. This law created dual jurisdiction between states and tribes that defers heavily to tribal governments.

TRIBAL GAMING

Without a doubt, Indian Tribal Gaming has sparked more controversy and created greater awareness about tribal sovereignty in the general public than any other Native American-related topic in recent years. The subject of Indian gaming will be more easily understood now that we've examined tribal sovereignty.

If a tribe decides to engage in casino gaming, the Indian Gaming Regulatory Act, or IGRA, controls these operations and requires that state governments must negotiate in good faith with tribes to form a compact, or agreement, that sets forth allowable games, limits and other terms. This law was passed in 1988 after the state of California tried to interfere with a tribe's attempt to open a gaming establishment there.

TRIBAL GAMING = STATE LOTTERIES

Indian tribes are not casino owners primarily. They are governments, which provide services to their citizens. So what a tribe therefore does with the revenue is very different than what the CEO of a big casino in Las Vegas or New Jersey would do with the money. Tribes use the revenues to benefit their members and run their governments.

What do governments do? They take care of the health of their community through health centers. They build schools and provide scholarships for higher education for their students. It is important for members of the general public to understand what the revenue is used for. Large tribes with large populations have to stretch that revenue pretty thin. Small tribes may be able to distribute a larger portion of their gaming revenues directly to tribal members.

Law enforcement agencies from local sheriffs all the way up to the FBI have investigated allegations that Indian gaming is a magnet for the mob or is run by shady characters from Jersey or Vegas. In every case, no links to organized crime were ever found. The Dept. of Justice has even stated that there is no evidence of any kind that organized crime has anything to do with Indian casinos.

Indian gaming is subject to more stringent regulation and security controls than any other type of gaming in the United States. IGRA sets forth the procedures and levels of this regulation. First is the tribal level. Each tribe has its own independent Tribal Gaming Commission to watch over operations within their tribe. The next level is state, through what's known as the tribal-state compacts. These are agreements between tribal governments and state governments on how the tribe will function within that state. (Many tribes strongly objected to this part of IGRA because it forced tribes to deal with state governments in spite of previous Supreme Court rulings.) Finally, there is federal regulation through the National Indian Gaming Commission and federal agencies such as the Dept. of Justice, the Treasury Dept. and the Dept. of the Interior.

As far as managing their casinos, each tribe operates its own gaming enterprise in the way that works best for them. Some manage their gaming property themselves, while others contract with outside management or gaming corporations to manage their casinos. In any case, the tribe always makes the final decisions.

According to Ernie Stevens Jr., Chairman of the National Indian Gaming Association,

"It goes back to the beginning of time when Indian people hold each other accountable. And we have a real strong ability to do that. The bottom line is we have to be accountable to our membership, and our tribal members demand accountability and integrity."

TAXATION

When it comes to money, people seem to have a lot of questions, like: "Do Indians pay taxes?" Individual Indian people pay all taxes required by state and federal laws. Individual Indians pay federal income tax, social security and FICA, as well as state income taxes. However, since it is illegal for one government to tax another, Indian tribal governments do not pay taxes to state governments or the federal government. A tribe does pay a percentage of its casino revenues to the state in which it operates as specified in their tribal-state compact, and that amount varies from state to state.

It is important to understand that only about <u>one-third</u> of tribes in the U.S. have any form of gaming, and the success of these operations varies widely. In fact, only twenty tribal casinos account for more than 50% of all Indian gaming revenues.

CURRENT STATUS OF TRIBAL SOVEREIGNTY

In summary, the U.S. government recognizes American Indian Tribes as domestic sovereign nations that possess self-government with certain limitations. Tribes have a nation-to-nation relationship with the U.S. federal government, and state governments generally do not have powers within reservations. Tribal sovereignty is seen by many as a paradox. While the U.S. government recognizes tribes as sovereign nations, Congress is recognized by the courts as having the right to limit sovereign powers to a certain degree. However, congressional power to do this has already been defined and restricted by the Supreme Court

For more information about any of the topics discussed in this booklet, visit any of the Internet sites listed in the bibliography or take a trip to the Indian reservation nearest you.

STUDY GUIDE

The outline of this booklet is as follows:

1.) Introduction/Tribes are governments.

2.) American Indians are America's First Inhabitants.

3.) Indian Tribes were considered pre-existing nations by Europeans.

4.) Sovereignty: the right to self-rule.

5.) Trust Responsibility.

6.) Sovereign Powers defined by Supreme Court rulings (1823-1832).

7.) Federally Recognized Tribes.

8.) Legislation that has modified Tribal Sovereignty:

   a. Indian Reorganization Act (1932)

   b. Public Law 280 (1953)

      c. Indian Self-Determination Act
         (1975)

      d. Indian Child Welfare Act (1978)

9.) Indian Gaming

      a. Indian Gaming Regulatory Act
         (1988)

      b. Differences between Tribal and
         Commercial Gaming

      c. Tribal Gaming Regulations &
         Operations

      d. Taxation and Revenues

10.) Conclusion: Current Status of Tribal
     Sovereignty

Suggested Activities

1. Using the Internet or maps available to you, locate the Indian Reservations closest to your location.

2. Have students do research on those tribes to learn about their history and culture.

3. Have students find out if any of those reservations have gaming operations.

4. Contact your state government or do an Internet search to see if you can obtain copies of the tribal-state compacts for gaming tribes in your area.

5. If possible, arrange a field trip to the nearest reservation or invite the tribe to send a representative to make a presentation about their history, culture and gaming operation.

Vocabulary Words/Concepts

Colonization: The process of a foreign power or nation taking over a region or other nation in order to rule that nation as a parent or controlling power.

Federal Recognition or Federally Recognized: A process whereby the federal U.S. government officially recognizes the legitimacy of a particular tribal government, which allows these tribes to enjoy certain rights and privileges as promised in treaties and legislation. There are approximately 550 federally recognized tribes in the U.S.

Gaming: The operation of a gambling establishment.

I.G.R.A.: Indian Gaming Regulatory Act (often spoken as a work pronounced: I-gruh) – a federal law passed in 1987 to define and regulate the Indian Gaming industry.

Nation: A group of people organized under one government, including American Indian tribes, recognized by other nations as having the right to interact with them on a government-to-government basis.

Rights: Powers, services and/or abilities due to someone by force of law or nature.

Sovereignty: 1) supremacy of rule or authority and 2) political autonomy. This can refer to an independent country or a form of government.

Supreme Court: Highest judicial authority in the United States.

Tribe: A system of social organization comprising several lineages and subgroups that share common ancestry, language, culture and name. American Indian tribes are considered to be ruled by their own governments.

U.S. Constitution: The fundamental document on which the United States is founded, which describes the rights of individuals and the laws that govern them.

Tribal-State Compact: A formal agreement between a tribal government and a state government. These agreements are required by IGRA in order for a tribe to be able to operate a casino.

Discussion Topics

Before reading the booklet, ask students to discuss what they know about these concepts:

- Sovereignty
- Tribes / Tribal Governments
- Domestic Dependent Nations
- Federally Recognized Tribes
- Trust Responsibility
- Indian Gaming
- Indian Gaming Regulations
- National Indian Gaming Commission

Conclusion

Sovereignty is the lifeblood of Native American tribal communities. American Indian people never laid claim of ownership to the lands they lived on, recognizing instead that they were an integral part of the cycle of life. To Native Americans, sovereignty is not possession of the land nor power or control over it. Simply put, sovereignty is a living relationship between the people, the land they live on and their right to determine how they use that land.

INFORMATION SOURCES

1. Dr. Katherine Spilde, formerly with the Center for California Native Nations.

2. Dr. John Johnson, Anthropologist, Santa Barbara Museum of Natural History.

3. DR. Jarrell C. Jackman, Santa Barbara Trust for Historic Preservation.

4. Dr. Eve Darian-Smith, Professor of Law & Society. UC-Santa Barbara.

5. Ernie Stevens Jr., Chairman, National Indian Gaming Association. Washington, DC.

6. Www.civilrights.org/indigenous/tribalsovereignty/

 ?referrer=https://www.google.com/

7. wikipedia.org/wiki/Tribal_sovereignty

8. Www.bia.gov/FAQs/

About the Author

Gary Robinson, a writer and filmmaker of Choctaw and Cherokee Indian descent, has spent more than twenty-five years working with American Indian communities to tell the historical and contemporary stories of Native peoples in all forms of media.

His television work has aired on PBS, Turner Broadcasting, Ovation Network, and others. His other non-fiction books, <u>From Warriors to Soldiers</u> and <u>The Language of Victory</u>, reveal little-known apsects of American Indian service in the U.S. military from the Revolutionary War to modern times.

He is also the author of seven teen novels in the *PathFinders* series published by Native Voices Books. This unique series features Native American teen main characters who go on adventures and rediscover the value of their own tribal identities.

His children's books include <u>Native American Night Before Christmas</u> and <u>Native American Twelve Days of Christmas</u>, published by Clearlight Books of Santa Fe.

He lives in rural central California. More information about the author can be found online at www.tribaleyeproductions.com and www.youtube.com/tribaleyepro. Follow him on Facebook at www.facebook.com/tribaleyepro.

Made in the USA
Columbia, SC
05 June 2021